HIGH FINANCE goes UPTOWN

STORY OF A BLACK OWNED BANK

ROGER **L. SMITH**

authorHOUSE®

AuthorHouse™
1663 Liberty Drive
Bloomington, IN 47403
www.authorhouse.com
Phone: 1 (800) 839-8640

As this story is told some of the names have been changed or omitted as not to identify any
particular person(s) or their position of employment assuming they were actually employed
there. This action was taken to protect the innocent. Some details may appear similar to
the events that may or may not have occurred but may have been embellished to heighten
the impact of the story, itself. Any such similarities may simply be coincidental.

Published by AuthorHouse 09/29/2017

ISBN: 978-1-5462-0675-0 (sc)
ISBN: 978-1-5462-0677-4 (hc)
ISBN: 978-1-5462-0676-7 (e)

Library of Congress Control Number: 2017913487

Print information available on the last page.

This book is printed on acid-free paper.

Contents

Dedication

I WANT TO EXPRESS MY SINCERE appreciation for those who made this book possible due to their relationship with the Bank or with me directly. Just to name a few, and to whom this book is dedicated, certainly, my biggest supporter, my wife, Patricia, who has supported me in every endeavor with absolute confidence, Babe I love you much. To my Mother, my Grandmother, my great-aunt Mama and two Aunts, (all deceased) whom I fondly refer to as the "Women in my life" for instilling in me the foundation of goodness, confidence and faith to try to live a productive life, no matter what. This book would not have been possible without the support and admiration of my children Lisa, Bryon and Christopher, and my Granddaughter, Jordan, who keep being amazed in my ability to accomplish this feat in spite of the odds working against me to accomplish this great endeavor. As well as, the mother of my children, Barbara and Elaine, whose love and dedication to them has nurtured them into wonderful productive citizens and the pride of our clan.

To all of those that worked at the Bank to help make success possible, a great "cloud of witnesses" too many to name, but yet they served with sterling dedication to the Bank and its success. I give special tribute to the Bank's Board of Directors and the various committees that oversaw the activities and gave 100% support to our "profit planning" ideas, creativeness and activities.

Finally, I want to thank my dear friends without whom my personal pursuits could not have been possible, Tom, Joe, Malcolm, Bill, Nat, Leroy, John, Irv, Oscar, Ernie, Al, Wayne, Randy, Ralph, Rev. Dr. W T Walker, Rev. Dr. C. Butts, Rev. Al, Mr. Bustamante, Nancy G., Reggie, Tony, Robert and many others who are not even aware of their contributions and many of their related businesses in New Jersey and New York that gave life to the dreams & this remarkable story in the life of a country boy from the small town of Cowpens, making his way to the big City. I thank God for all and any that gave breath to this endeavor, knowingly or unknowingly, on purpose or by accident, to God I give the Glory. I would be remiss if I did not thank my deceased friend, Brother Freddie, who gave me constant "wise council" on many occasions and his loving wife, "D" and their family. To my immediate family, my two brothers, Joe and Fred; my sister, Vivian and a host of nephews, nieces, cousins and wonderful in-laws especially Garvin. I love you all very much more than you could ever love me back.

I give special tribute to the many unsung heroes and she-roes, those that go about their work with commitment and devotion to which many of the significant accomplishments by named others could not have been possible. Those unrecognized warriors who worked or served in the background, not seeking fortune or fame, and stayed far from the limelight, yet instead gave of their time and talents unselfishly, so that others may stand in the forefront with their minutes of fame. Finally, I would be remiss again if I did not pay tribute to the many teachers from a variety of schools, that I attended namely, Golden Street Kindergarten and Mary H. Wright Elementary of Spartanburg, S.C. Ralph Bunche Elementary of Cowpens, Roosevelt Village Elementary and Booker T. Washington Jr. High School of Columbia, Benjamin E. Mays High School of Pacolet, S.C. I give special tribute to Mrs. Rogers, Mr. Owens, Mrs. Miller, Mrs. Smalls, Mr. Williams, Mrs. Mitchell, Mrs. White, Mr. Brown, Mr. Blanding, Mr. Brockman, Coach Patrick and Littlejohn, and a host of many others that through their dedication, devotion and professionalism in addition to their teaching methods laid the groundwork for this significant achievement. Together with my Schoolmates, especially Sterling and other supportive schoolmates from A to Z, who challenged me, encouraged me and supported me to be the best that I can be in spite of the lack of proper educational materials and supplies. I dare not forget to mention the cornerstone of my desire and thirst to excel, Morehouse College and Dr.

B. E. Mays, then President, Farleigh Dickerson University, New York University, Interdenominational Theology Center (ITC), Grand Canyon University, Newburgh Theological Seminary. All played and continue to play a major role in my career pursuits, especially again Morehouse College, the anchor of my thirst. Praises to GOD for the many blessings!!!! Finally, but certainly not the least of these, The Lord God Almighty, who preserved me and blessed me beyond measure and my imagination with additional chances to get it right before going on home to Glory, I thank God for Jesus Christ and his grace and mercy. In addition to my spiritual and prayer partner, "Carp" and other old and new friends that I chat with or text often in continuing to wish each other well in our future.

I hope lastly, that you will gleam as much pleasure in reading this material as I had in writing it and provide some if not many, a desire to excel in spite of the odds working against them. Dare to dream that touching the sky is within reach, and not dreaming beyond your immediate expectations is a tragedy. Your future is in your hands, and trust in the God, from whom all blessings flow, but get busy and take advantage of the "opportunities" which sometimes come masquerading as "hard work".

Thanks to all my friends in the Clergy and co-laborers in The Gospel of Jesus Christ. My fellow Seminarians and brilliant Professors at the famed Seminary I T C that I attend and I shall be dedicated to their principles and standards of excellence. They are leading and guiding us along the way in preparing us for the promise. Please continue to pray for me as I pray for you because GOD is not finished with us yet. I thank all of you for your love, your prayers and your loyal support throughout my journey.

A Special Acknowledgement

I MUST EXPRESS HOMAGE TO STEVE Harvey for his prayers when he prayed over me (as I was told) when I collapsed after suffering a massive stroke in Birmingham, Alabama. I was scheduled to make a guest appearance on the Steve Harvey Morning Show to promote The Annual Black Classic Football weekend in 2009. This Annual Classic had been sponsored for several years by the local Golden Corral Restaurants owned by Minority businessman, Joe Wilson. This year Steve Harvey had been invited down as the "special guest performer" for the weekend along with some performing musical groups. We must all keep in mind that the power of prayer lies in the One who hears it and not all in the one who says it. Let us always pray for one another. Thank you Mr. Harvey and may GOD continue to bless you and yours beyond measure as you continue to pass on the many blessings to others in need and in deeds as evidence of your caring and God's promises. Peace be with you, My Brother, Glory to GOD in the highest.

Introduction

THIS BOOK IS NOT THE HISTORY of any particular Bank, but simply one of the stories about a Bank that could be told by many of its dedicated employees and staff of about 60 employees during the early 80's at the peak of the Bank's success. Certainly to the Bank's Board of Directors, we certainly owe a tremendous debt of gratitude for their commitment and support to the Minority Community for fostering small business endeavors. Perhaps even a few customers could give testimony as to the metamorphism of the Bank after I arrived there, as it relates to their experience with the little bank located in Any town in America not far from a famous movie theater in that area of Town. Even though I was there just a little over 2 years, I believe that my fingerprint is all over Minority Banking Institutions nationwide, even today.

I have come to realize as I enter the twilight of my years that unless you tell your story, it can easily become someone else's story or his-story, and that story may be totally different than what actually happened during those years. Fortunately, the facts don't change and what was true and accurate then, remains true and accurate today. Perhaps this book may even answer some questions that have remained unanswered for far too many years. It is certainly my hope to shed some light on the small Bank in a popular City with a talented few bankers that made a great impact as it reached a pinnacle of high achievement in its history and changed Minority Banking throughout the Country and time. On many articles regarding Minority Banks and their ultimate demise, you only read about mismanagement and bad loans. A story that is not only familiar with Minority Banks but many other Bank failures nationwide. But in the case of this Bank, there were many successes within the Bank's history. I believe that this "Bank" brought the best talent available to be found in any small Bank, Majority or Minority of that time. We had exceptional top level management talent and a loan portfolio that comprised of mostly Fortune 500 Companies.

This publication, for one thing, is intended to shed some light on the Bank's significant achievements that gave Minority Banks credibility in the marketplace. I believe that through my direct actions and those that supported these efforts at the Bank made its greatest strides and had direct impact that made great success even possible. The Bank received its greatest success in financial standing and reputation during those few years that I was employed there. We operated with professionalism and a talented middle management crew and other employees that developed under my direct tutoring that was second to none. We made the key decisions and recommendations toward its ultimate success with the proper guidance and clear documentation toward policy, principles and profitability. Even by today's standards, there has never been a talented team that came together to equal or surpass the skills that our Management group possessed and set the bar in achieving the milestones that were set. We could not have achieved our goals without the support of all our employees, each and every one of them dedicated to excellence. We salute them all and the work that all of us contributed toward its success throughout time. It was their love and dedication to high achievement that nurtured them into wonderful productive employees and supportive community advocates.

Chapter 1

In the Beginning

THE STORY DOES NOT BEGIN WITH me but with some dedicated famous heroes and heroines, a famous baseball player and his wife, and a famous boxer and his wife, a Civil Rights advocate & M L King, Jr. lieutenant and neighborhood clergy, a magazine publisher and owner, several Black Executives that held top positions with major Fortune Companies, a local Real Estate Management Firm, a community activist and a National Media Network pioneer and a host of others interested in economics and Community development.

There was much work to be done in transforming an entire neighborhood and mindset and there were many successes along their journey. The job done by those that preceded our group, kept pace with the ever-changing banking environment. Then we arrived and assumed the task of taking the Bank to the next level and the responsibility to maintain and stabilize the Bank's viability and competiveness within the marketplace. There were extreme difficult times of turmoil and uncertainty lying ahead for us although unknown at that time. Those early Bankers were "care takers" and maintained the Bank until we, the talented few, came aboard. I certainly don't know any of the specifics that those early bankers endured but being in the heart of the financial center, I realize that competition was keen and brisk. Unfortunately, I am not privileged to those times or instances that preceded me, but only with the financial condition of the Bank when I arrived there in the early 1980's.

I had become friends with a classmate in Graduate School while working on my Master's Degree in Bank Management. He was the President of a local Minority Bank and had mentioned several times of another Minority Bank where I might find opportunities there with my talents and abilities. I must admit that I wasn't familiar with that particular Bank at the time until I met its President at several business functions and seminars for minority businesses in the City. Eventually, the President of that Bank and I had an occasion to discuss the Bank and its potential. There was an immediate opening for a V P in branch operations, heading up their several branches in which the branch managers would report to that office. I was somewhat reluctant even though my training and background was extensive in branch banking from several large financial institutions which was quite significant and impressive. I had worked for one of the top major Banks in the Country where I reported to the V P in charge of 20 or so branches located in the heart of the financial center after I had completed an extensive Management Training Program and which included branch banking experiences. My responsibilities at that time included preparing reports on branch operations and ranking them according to profitability and staffing, in addition to teaching seminars, and interacted with Top Management. Later I left that Bank to become a Branch Manager for a major Bank in another State at a very tender age (24) years of age. There I restructured the bank's operations and restored it to profitability, even though the original plan was to close that particular location due to the lack of earnings for many years. They eventually built a new branch building at that location. I was able to secure that opportunity based upon the fact that the Bank was located near the headquarters of a notable Civil Rights Activist, Author and local hero. However, my response to the President of the Bank to that job offer was a counter proposal. Although I knew that I could do that job very well, my counter offer was that I would take that job offer only if after correcting that situation that I could take over the Commercial Loan Department of the Bank. I felt that my skills were better suited there and that I could have the greatest impact on the Bank's bottom line earnings in the Commercial Loan area. We couldn't agree on that proposition because he already had someone in that position and he wasn't ready to make any changes there. I was already in a very comfortable position for several years with a major Bank where I was responsible for small business lending, which included SBA type loans and other lending for the entire State and I served on several loan committees for major bank lending responsibilities. In addition to that, the bank was paying for my graduate studies in Banking, plus I also represented the Bank at various business and social functions involving the local community and businesses. Further, I also served on several Boards, including United Way, Federal Executive Boards, etc. In other words, I didn't really need to make any moves at all, except that I wanted to bring my masterful skills and Banking talents to The Minority Banking Community. Eventually, maybe after about 6 months or so later, that Bank's President called me and we finally had a meeting of the minds and I made the decision to join the Bank as V P in charge of commercial or Business Lending. However, I didn't know it at the time but the Bank could not make loans. Therefore, my first priority, then became to write a loan policy that could be accepted by the Regulatory Authority, both Federal and State. Such a

5

loan policy would enable the Bank to then make loans but such a policy had to be detailed in procedures, i.e. about how to properly handle loan request, receiving the correct documentation, analyzing the information received for loan consideration and analyzed to write-up for presentation to the proper channels at the Bank. When I joined the Bank the existing loan portfolio consisted of loans on the books shared by other Major Banks, but it was not adequate to sustain operations to help the Bank's earnings and cash flow. The total loan portfolio was approximately 13 million dollars, and the Bank was struggling to stay afloat and using tax loss carry forwards to help stay afloat.

No loan staff existed presently and it was difficult to recruit qualified bankers to work there because specific skills and talents were needed to help build a successful loan portfolio and offer a career path and an enhancement to banking skills. Once you worked there, in your next career move you would have to be able to demonstrate marketable skills because the Bank was not widely known nor noted for talented personnel.

Because of this and other reasons, it was a common practice for Bank Executives to be on leave from their perspective employers when joining the Bank on a temporary basis and based on the uncertainty of how employment would work out there, fall back on their options to return to their previous jobs. I understand this consideration because one had to protect their financial future. Ultimate career success in Banking like most other careers is never a sure thing even if the Bank is successful. In other words, when and if things got too difficult there, they could leave and go back to their perspective Bank of employment. It was normal in those cases for some to have employment contracts which locked them in for only a specific period of time with very lucrative pay grades. This Bank, however, was one of the Nation's largest Black Banks according to size at that time.

I ultimately joined the Bank without a contract and without a commitment to return to my previous employer. I was solely dependent on my success there at the Bank and I had the upmost confidence in my ability to turn the Bank around and make the Bank successful and profitable. Then and only then I could be judged purely by my performance and merits of those achieved there at the Bank. My original goal was to eventually become President of a Bank even though I had never really met a Bank President until my arrival in that City some years ago as a Trainee for one of the major Bank's in the Financial district direct from my years at College. My long range goal was to start my own Bank, The Smith National Bank. This job would certainly put me on track to accomplish one of those goals or perhaps both but only if I was successful. Although I was very excited about the opportunity to work at there, I still had no clue as to what to expect as I arrived there on my first day of employment. I knew that I was joining a team of seasoned bankers from other major lending institutions and we were expected to purge our skills in making the Bank operate better. I was becoming one of several Vice Presidents there at the Bank and was placed in charge of Commercial (business) Loans or Lending. While at my previous position in the other Bank's loan area, I had a staff of one but she was more than a secretary or an assistant, she was actually a good friend. Even though we had developed a bond over the years, I did not ask her to make the move to this new position with me in another City, mainly because I didn't think she wanted to go there and I didn't want to be rejected. Her position with me was her first job out of business school. Therefore, I chartered out on this journey alone but very confident in spite of some others questioning my decision, if it was actually a correct one. I was enjoying a primary position in that very popular and noteworthy Bank by being the Bank's representative at business functions and attending Banking functions as a key Officer in charge. Now the thought of being one of among a group of many and not necessarily the primary decision maker was not an idea of progress in the mind of some of my friends and others. In spite of this, I remained excited and confident in the future although it remained unknown.

In all thy ways acknowledge him, and he shall direct thy paths. Prov. 3:-6

CERTIFICATE of PROMOTION

Golden Street Kindergarten

This certifies that: Roger Lee Smith is qualified to be promoted from the

Pre-School Department Kathlyn Frances Jackson Teacher

Chapter 2

Obsticles as Opportunities

I WAS TOLD BY A FRIEND much wiser than I, a spiritually anointed person that I have known for many years and respect very much for his honesty and candor said that this story, according to his analysis, actually began much sooner than I realized. Perhaps even as early as my initial years at Morehouse College, in Atlanta, Georgia. It was during my freshman year of study when there was no thought of a career in Banking and didn't even have any money to open a bank account and ultimately opened my first account as a savings account to be used as a source to cash my pay check after getting my first job with H J Russell Construction Company there in Atlanta.

I was in College on a Benjamin E. Mays Scholarship and yet had no money before finding a job. Therefore I had to devise a system of study which included borrowing my roommate's books based upon his study habits, since I didn't have books for my classes or money to purchase any books. My roommate and I took the same basic courses during our first semester, the specific courses that were assigned to us. My roommate also had the only television on the third floor of Graves Hall and the other students would stop by and spend time watching T V programs most of the time. Therefore my roommate would spend the early evening hours studying until the late hours at night. I would spend those same hours sleeping and upon his return to the room, I would get up, borrow his textbooks and go study until the wee hours of the morning, sometimes even all night. On those occasions when I would study all night until breakfast time even though I didn't have a meal ticket to eat breakfast. On those occasions and several others, I would use my roommate's meal ticket book since he didn't get up early or eat breakfast or even some other meals. Unfortunately, on many occasions that would be my only meal of the day.

The next semester, due to our change in schedules and our different fields of study as Major concentrations, our class courses were different and therefore I could not use my roommate's textbooks any longer. My method of study had to change abruptly. For most of my other classes, new editions of the textbooks were being used; therefore, I would go to the library and study from the previous older editions of those same textbooks. Most of the time, I would end up in the stacks, the attic of the library, spending the night, studying related assignments from the old textbooks. These developments highlighted my freshman and sophomore years at Morehouse College and almost led to my losing my scholarship because of poor grades. During my sophomore year my grades continued to suffer as a result of my not being adequately prepared for College classroom duty, to the extent that I thought that my scholarship was in jeopardy.

When I arrived there, like some other students,

my reading skills were not adequate for College work. Fortunately, Morehouse College offered remedial reading classes that were taught in trailers on campus that brought to us different methods to improve our reading skills. I took advantage of every opportunity that was offered to improve my skills development. Still I was concerned about flunking out of School. I approached a homeboy, an upper classman in whom I had much respect, the only one there from my hometown and High School, Terry, to solicit his advice concerning my future plans about continuing my study there at "Morehouse" due to my failing grades. I remember the advice that he gave to me and it made a profound difference in my approach to staying in school there. He responded by advising me that even if I wasn't getting the grades that I felt that I deserved, the main thing that he asked was if I "was learning anything"? That was the primary reason for my being there for education and that was to learn. My response was a resounding "yes". He responded by saying that the grades will come if I was indeed learning anything.

However, there was still the issue of losing my scholarship because of my poor grades during my study there. The other person that I needed to speak to was the President of the College, Dr. Benjamin E. Mays. In speaking with him, he placed his arms around my shoulders and promptly assured me that my scholarship was not in jeopardy as long as he was the President there at Morehouse College. Actually, that was like "God" reassuring me that all would be well, and what a relief that was and a sense of comfort with some tensions removed almost immediately. From that time on going forward, I was able to concentrate on my studies and really enjoy campus life, and at one point even made the Dean's List while playing College Football, a sport that I had never played before. One of my big issues was going to class but by playing football I had extra time to do my assignments due to our out of town travel schedules.

Now, back to my job assignment at my new place of employment, there were no written job descriptions available for most of the employees at the time that I arrived there but were surely needed for the employees. The main objective therefore was to simply notice a job undone and just do it, if you knew how. I was really excited about starting my new career and my first day was most unusual. I drove to work in my recently acquired Mercedes Benz, a pearl white 4 door coupe, when most other Bankers there were driving Fords and Chevys. However, on my first day drive in from the nearby State, I actually missed my proper exit off the Parkway and exited a few blocks farther away. Not wanting to be late for my first day, I was looking for the correct street to make a proper U turn and noticed an attractive young lady at the street corner. Being very caution and not wanting to appear unwise to City affairs, when summoned by the young lady, I eased over to her street side curb and only lowered my window slightly. Since it was only around seven-thirty or so (7:30 A. M.), I assumed that she wanted directions, although I was lost myself, I was perfectly willing to offer my assistance in any reasonable way that I could. She leaned down with a lovely smile and attractive features and promptly asked "do you want some head before you go to the office?" I was in total disbelief and shocked but somehow I was able to remain composed as I respond very quickly to appear to be accustomed to such propositions, I responded by saying "how much will it cost?" Upon her response, which appeared reasonable, I said that I would return later on at lunch, naturally I didn't but certainly was a most unusual way to start the day and a new career.

The type of car that I drove gave me instant acceptability, almost celebrity status among the neighborhood crew who volunteered to watch my car when I worked late after hours at nights and on week-ends. Back to my job assignment at the Bank, since there were only a few if any written job descriptions that existed at the time, everyone did according to their desires which left major task undone creating customer unrest and dissatisfaction. Another main objective was then deciding what jobs could be done based upon experience and bank knowledge and their aptitude to learn how to perform new task through my tutoring and outside sources of training for bank employees. There was much work to be done even from basic banking foundations which caused me to wonder what task or duties had been undertaken to strengthen the staff prior to my arrival.

Upon my arrival at the Bank, it was an older structure not well maintained where management offices were on the main level with some upstairs. I was promptly introduced to the Management staff which consisted of the President, a V P & Controller, a V P of Operations, an Exe. V P and then I assumed a role in the team. Much later during my tenure, we were joined by a very competent and talented staff attorney as a Vice President and legal counsel with a tremendous banking background in the areas of Banking. I might add that was a brilliant move since we were outsourcing all of our legal work which was quite expensive. I would say very confidently, that we comprised the most talented group of Bankers to be located at any Bank, Minority or Majority at that time. We were the original "Fabulous Five", the "Fab 5", we countered the age old argument that "Black

Banks" could not afford to hire good talent. As a matter

of fact, during my tenure, we disproved a number of myths

about Black Banks and Bankers as you will see later in this

reading.

	1st 6 Wks.	2nd 6 Wks.	3rd 6 Wks.	Exam.	1st Sem. Av.	4th 6 Wks.	5th 6 Wks.	6th 6 Wks.	Exam.	2nd Sem. Av.	Yearly Av.
Days Absent	1	0	0			0	3				
Days Tardy											
Conduct	B-C	B	B	78-80		C	B	B			B
English	A	B-	A	78	90	B	B	A	95	93	92
Bus. Math.	A	A	A	68	88	A	A	A	100	99	94
Algebra II	B+B-	A	96	94	A	B-	A	99	96	95
Economics	A	A	A	92	94	A	A	A	98	95	95
Basic Math.	A	A	A	100	97	A	A	A	100	99	97

Chapter 3

Changing of the Guard/ New Strategies

WHEN I JOINED THE BANK, IT was not permitted to make any loans due to ill-advised loans that had been made without the benefit of a viable Loan Policy being in place to detail and determine repayment ability or establish guidelines for lending. Therefore my first priority on the new job as told by the Bank's President was to write a loan policy that would permit the Bank to lend money accordingly to the rules and regulations of the Federal Banking Regulators under which we operated. The Board of Directors were a very diverse group of individuals, consisting of religious clergy, community activist, officers of financial institutions, insurance companies, real estate management agency and media personnel and including print and voice channels. All of these factors and many others played a key role in the Banks growth and success, along with the dedicated staff of individuals.

Further, we had no loan department staff to which help build a viable loan portfolio or to manage loans or lending practices. Therefore after several months of developing and writing an approved Loan Policy, the next step was to develop a staff to manage the loan operations with job descriptions. During those days I felt very comfortable doing my own recruiting since I knew very well the type of candidates or employees that were needed to be effective in the positions that were required. I did not rely on the traditional Human Resource Department or staff personnel for hiring or soliciting candidates because our needs were very specific in nature. Actually, this was better for me because I knew what specific skills and abilities that were required to complete the establishment of a functional Commercial loan Department to blend in with an accounting area that was functioning adequately. I went out to the various major banks in the City recruiting the right individuals with the necessary skills that would fit the structure for a productive loan division and fit in with the existing employee mix. This proved to be a very difficult task, even though the City was a mecca for financial minded seasoned recruits, even much more difficult than I had first imagined due to the specific skills that were required. In other words, I found many candidates that was willing to make a job change because they were unhappy where they were and wanted more money but lacked the necessary skills that the Bank needed. A good number of individuals were simply not that familiar with the Bank. I found many who wanted to work for the Bank for greater pay but really had little or none of the skills that were really needed for the Bank's ultimate success. My first recruit was an individual that worked for one of the Major larger banks that had an excellent reputation for lending practices. I had even taken a lending course at that particular Bank, myself a few years ago. His training and background was a perfect fit for us in our present state of affairs. I offered him an Officer title and a position as Jr. Loan Officer and direct responsibility for certain loans that we were to develop and he became the first hire as I began to staff my department with able and talented individuals. Next, we needed a loan analyst to do the write-ups on loan request that was familiar with analyzing financial statements and working on spread sheets. I recruited a senior analyst from another Major Bank after realizing that he knew how to analyze financials and taught him the new format that we were using when reviewing and analyzing the company's financials and the new guidelines for loan presentations to the Loan Committee for consideration and approval. Another experienced employee joined us as a loan officer as well and now finally, we were ready to start soliciting loans and operating effectively. These new recruits were hired as an Officers of the Bank, as well as several other new hires were brought onboard that provided a nearly complete staff but quite adequate for our purposes at the time.

One of my many surprises was observing the Bank's financial projections for the upcoming periods. The Bank was operation on an old Budget operating format, in other words similar to a non-profit organization. In this format "post it notes" were being used and left behind on various places to remember to turn off the lights when leaving a room, all activities were done to keep expenses down to the minimum, concentrating on holding down expenses to become profitable and not concentrating on earning revenue. My initial focus was to change the "mindset" of my colleagues to profit making pursuits and not an emphasis on concentration on holding expenses down. My next immediate task was to change their emphasis and their plans and objectives to thoughts of "Profit Planning" strategies and establish a Monthly Report on our goals to projected earnings as our operating guide and primary focus. Further, we would provide periodic financial reports providing updates to the Board of Directors as to where we were in relationship to our planning for profitability goals. We were poised and ready to do some REAL banking business for a change. Now READY, SET, GO!!!!!

While I thought that we were now posed to do business, the employee morale was very low. Apparently there were many issues directly affecting the employees and their working conditions that were being ignored or simply not being addressed adequately. Everyone was too busy putting out fires to concentrate on improvements in the working areas of the Bank, folk were very busy. One day I noticed that of a water fountain that was inoperable. The fountain spout did not operate properly, the force of water could not reach high enough for the employees to get a proper drink of water. This was brought to my attention by one of the employees since I was not a water drinker myself. They were complaining about being thirsty. I immediately set out to correct this situation but realizing that a repair was not the best option cost wise after getting several estimates. I ordered a system that brought in fresh bottled water for drinking. Unfortunately I got in a little trouble with upper management of the Bank because

I did not seek prior approval for this expenditure. I simply saw a need and since the problem had existed for quite a while without being addressed, I simply took care of it. After expressing disapproval, I was informed that this monthly cost would be charged to my departmental budget. The benefits in this case certainly outweighed the penalty and greatly improved employee morale. The cost of this monthly service was minimum compared to the abundance of benefits to the overall moral to the employees overall. Especially those that had a desire for fresh cool drinking water. There were other issues that I was able to address due to my concern and care for the employee issues and I took the opportunity to correct them or at least show some interest for their well-being as employees. It goes without saying that employee morale was moving to an all-time high, we were heading in the right direction earnings wise. All of the employees were dedicated and loyal to the Bank but simply needed direction, guidance and proper supervision. I found no problem in getting the staff to preform once they understood their assignments. I gave and received proper respect and cooperation in every situation was demonstration and our expressed concern for the individual was mutual. If you learn to love the people and teach the Banking experience, then that posture has been proven to work effectively.

As I was preparing to attend my first Loan Committee meeting but only as an interested observer just to see how the Bank presented its loans for review and approval process. To my surprise, I noticed two of the Senior Officers standing outside the meeting room just prior to going inside, pumping and hitting each other similar to football players before the big game, pounding each other on their chest and shoulders. I inquired as to what was taking place there? They responded by informing me that they were preparing for a battle, there's a war going on and we needed to be aggressive and ready for combat in order to go to war and compete. Since this was my first meeting I mostly remained silent but took mental notes as to the specifics of the things that happened there inside the meeting room. I watched as an argument ensued and almost developed into a fist fight when one of the committee members stood up and challenged another to combat. I realized that this was not the way that Bank Credit Committees should be conducted. There was too much animosity and nothing would really be accomplished unless we were organized and all working together on the same page. These meetings lasted for 2 to 3 hours and in most instances nothing was ever done or accomplished. The meetings begin with the Banking Officials bringing in several boxes of files for presentations and upon questions asked, one would commence rumbling through the boxes for answers which represented totally unpreparedness for this type of duty. Upon reflecting on my previous experience with loan committees some of which I was a member at those meetings when I was with other Banks, mostly all of them took place in the day time during regular business hours. Accordingly none of this conduct was apparent nor condoned at any of those meetings.

After some deliberation, I realized that since our meetings were in the evenings after normal working hours, many of the participants were missing their dinner plus not being at home with their families. My solution was to order food for Committee members to have a snack before the meeting started in hopes to ease some of the tension which prevailed therein. I had sandwiches catered from a local deli along with side items and beverages. You cannot even imagine the major difference that food served made in the continued deliberations of our Credit Committee meetings in a very favorable manner. A few members even came early to dine and review the loans that were to be presented to the committee in the new format which was several typed sheets outlining the company's financials with write-ups on repayment, for an approval vote. After this adjustment and the manner in which the new procedure in the revision of the way in which the loans were presented thoroughly, the meetings were conducted with promptness and civility and then all the meeting ran smooth and without difficulty. During this period, we never received a decline vote from any loan presented before the Committee for almost a two-year period. We were prepared and presented our information in clear detailed and a precise manner. I advised those other Officers that we were not in combat but were a sales and marketing team for the Bank's profitability. That our job was to prepare ourselves adequately, do our homework and market the loans as a profitable source for business potential for the Bank.

There was another major undertaking that led to the Bank becoming the stellar Financial Institution that it became in those few short years that I was there. My Superior, the Exe. V P approached me about a problem that had developed with a loan with a major Fortune 500 Company. We were the lead Bank in a participation loan with a group of Minority Banks. He stated to me that one of the smaller participating Banks had misplaced their original signed note of $50,000 and needed a replacement note to be signed by the Corporate Treasurer of that Fortune 500 Company. Naturally the Company's legal department had got involved and wanted disclaimers, hold harmless agreements, etc. and a host of other legal requirements, in order to have a duplicate note signed. My initial response was why did all these Banks have their own notes when it was not necessary or required for the Banks to participate. The response was "this is the way it has always been done" and required for them to be a loan participant in the lending consortium. I was informed that they would not participate unless they had a note evidencing their loan participation because they were accustomed to only doing it that way. I knew that this was not the way larger banks made participation loans because I had been involved in many of them in my previous positions with other Banks. This method was antiquated and no longer in use by progressive lending institutions and should have been discontinued. The Minority Banks had a Minority Loan Consortium Program in which we could offer major credit accommodations to Fortune 500 Companies. While these Loans were supported solely by Minority Banks, however the present structure or format of the Program made it very difficult and cumbersome in that each participating Bank had to produce their own note in the package of closing documents. Therefore the CFO or Treasurer might end up signing some thirty (30) or so unnecessary documents at each closing which made the proposal less marketable, unattractive and unacceptable. I looked over one of these deals and immediately knew there was a better way and it was our duty as the lead Bank to show other similar banks a better way of doing business.

After reviewing the process and I was able to recommend a change in the Program by having the Corporate representative sign only one (1) note with that of the Lead Minority Bank and then send Participation Agreements for each Bank to sign evidencing their participation and the amount of their participation. This process would replace their own note and eliminate their need to have their own Bank's individual note. I presented a copy of a draft of a "participation agreement" for review and approval from the other Officers of our Bank and for those of other participating Banks. This new format was already being used by many larger Majority Banking

Institutions without any issues. Once approved, we were geared up to move forward with this new procedural format. However, a few Minority Banks that were not familiar with this concept refused to accept this new procedure and lost the opportunity to participate in these loans and improve their profitability Fortunately, there were several Hispanic Banking Institutions to fill the gap, in order to make our concept more marketable and acceptable in the marketplace. This proved to be a stroke of genius because this enabled the Minority Bank Consortium Loan Program to build itself more substantially into a great marketable tool with those Fortune 500 Companies that were desirous to do business with Minority Banks. This program became the prime money maker for the Bank and propelled the Bank to new profit levels never achieved before and ultimately we became the number one Black Bank in the Nation in profitability. The Wall Street Journal named us the leader in average ratio in ROA than any Bank Citywide; we must have been doing something right.

On other occasions, as we were building the Loan Portfolio in small business loans within the Communities in which we served. The Bank had four branches throughout the City We made the first loan ever to Hale House, a non-profit that had been using Federal Funds and Grants to fund its operations adequately. A local Restaurant and two oil pioneers from a nearby area, a female electrical contractor that was doing business with the City, also a female temporary employment agency that had prestige Fortune 500 Companies as their client base. We were thriving and so was our business community, this was what those pioneer organizers had in mind when they formed the Bank. There was still much work to be done especially within our communities and staffing needs. Many of our small businesses that could possible qualify for loans were lacking adequate bookkeeping and accounting support. There were several Minority C P A Accounting Firms located within the City and I met with one of them that agreed to assist us as we attempted to development a small business loan portfolio within the Bank.

Roger L. Smith
Benjamin E. Mays H.S.
Pacolet, S.C,.
Class of '64.

Roger L. Smith
Morehouse College
Atlanta< GA
Class of '68.

Chapter 4

Building Blocks/ Making it Big in the City

WE WERE HAVING GOOD SUCCESS AND the Bank's reputation in financial circles and elsewhere were growing favorably. I was meeting many interesting young enterprising talented individuals, even some successful entertainers were contacting the Bank in the hope of doing business including Sammy Davis, Jr., and successful song writers that wrote for Roberta Flack, Bill Withers and the like. A young executive from C B S Records that was producing shows throughout the Country including a concert with Ray Charles at a popular entertainment Center and Barry White on a national tour in 10 cities throughout the Country. A Millionaire from

New Jersey introduced by a prominent New Jersey Defense Attorney contacted us as his business was expanding as was our reputation spreading across State lines. In addition, the distinguished Reverend Al stopped by to assist us in getting deposits from The Entertainment Industry particular the recording companies. The President of the Bank assigned me to work directly with The Goodly Reverend as we called on the various recording companies including C B S Records. Among all these activities there was an occasion to meet with the key executive from a major charge/credit card company. This association led to the Bank issuing the first Minority Bank major credit card that had a line of credit attached to it, as a prestige Gold Card with the Bank's name on it. We then developed a banking product called "The Prestige Banker" which included a interest bearing DDA account with overnight investments, the Prestige Credit-card Gold Card and other customer perks, no waiting in long lines, however it required that customers maintain a minimum $10,000 deposit. There were numerous other plans on the drawing board that offered many challenges but the benefit of an abundance of rewards in profits and reputation. In times of great difficulty and turmoil, opportunities are present for tremendous success and we made excellent use of our chances.

We were trying to build our loan portfolio and design new products for our customer base in the process. We couldn't just duplicate what the other much larger competitive banks were doing and simply try to out-market them with their vast resources. Our main task was to develop products primarily for our targeted market which was the Minority Community. By attending a number of business Expos and Seminars we were able to meet many interesting business persons that had ideas about benefiting the Bank' growth and make money One deal became very interesting that required further analysis, my immediate supervisor, was very good at detailing complicated concepts to a simple breakdown of very complex issues. I was good at conceptionalizing or grasping the idea or concepts but those ideas had to be broken down or written into layman's terms for Board approvals. One very important deal required a journey out to another borough of the City to visit a mortgage company that was looking for a line of credit to underwrite more mortgages for investment proposes. We reviewed the mortgage company and their warehouse where documentation for submitting packages of made mortgages for mortgage-backed securities for investment were being held. After reviewing the process we were able to provide a line of credit for $1 million dollars for the acquisition of V A and F H A mortgages to be converted into Ginny Mae Mortgage Backed Securities. We had pre-arranged a pre-purchase agreement of these securities once issued through H U D by a major Wall Street firm. Our earnings of these investments were significant enough to propel our Bank into the top earnings Minority Bank in the Country. They were so significant that Wall Street investment bankers took notice and wanted to know who was this little Minority Bank and what were they doing. The Bank's name was listed on major investment securities and even banking regulators took notice and made appointments to visit us for questioning for possible violations of banking regulations. We were given a timetable for a visit by the Federal Regulatory Agency which gave us time to get our position papers in order along with our very capable legal counsel that had a banking regulatory background which helped us tremendously in the preparation of defending our position.

As the Comptroller of The Currency of the Federal Reserve System of the Eastern Division of the United States met in that early morning session, we presented a diagram of how the Mortgage-backed Security Program functioned at our Bank. After some discussions and several breaks for refocusing on our strategy, we were able to present the following scenario; the Bank we would fund or purchase FHA or VA Mortgages in $100,000 increments for our $1 million dollar portfolio for resale to investors. We had an arrangement with a brokerage firm on a pre-purchase of the Security document for investment once it was issued and prepared for delivery from H U D to the Brokerage firm as an investment instrument. The Frm would then wire our money upon delivery of said security. This was a big money maker for the Bank and helped propelled us into the top earnings Minority Bank in the Country. The Regulatory Agency accused us of making loans beyond our legal lending limit which was about $600,000 at that time and these transactions were all $1 Million each. We argued back and forth that these transactions were not in violation of the Bank's legal lending limits since they were not loans as such but simply investments fully insured or guaranteed by the Federal Government as F H A mortgages or V A loans and therefore exempt from Federal regulations of loans. therefore if any one of the loans defaulted during the conversion process, another loan could be substituted in its place in order to keep the investment intact. We would do several of these a month and the earnings from those transactions allowed us to become the first Minority Bank (Black) to earn $ 1 Million dollar in a year. These Securities were being issued with the Bank's name on them, which drew the attention of the entire investment community, we were truly representing High Finance in our area uptown.

We presented our case before the Banking Authorities; our in-house legal Council was brilliant and in step by step with me as we presented our augment for continuing these transactions. After a long detail of extensive questions and rebuttals, they left to take the matter under advisement for reconsideration at their corporate offices and to advise us accordingly in the near future. The augment that we presented again and again was that while these amounts exceeded our legal lending limit for making loans, these transactions were not actually loans but investments and since these documents, mortgages were all insured or guaranteed by the Federal Government, we were not at "risk" for these amounts. They were simply risk-free investments, even if one of those mortgage loans defaulted in the process, it could be replaced or substituted by one that was current. Our hopes were running high that we could continue this profitable business venture, there were some thoughts that we would be issued a "cease and desist" order to refrain from this activity. After several weeks of waiting the official response and anticipating favorable notifications it came from the Department of the Currency, stating ...a favorable opinion "that we could continue this type of business as in a routine manner". In these unfamiliar settings we had to carve out opportunities where none previously existed. These situations presented to be problems and our creativeness provided solutions that were extremely profitable for the Bank. In other words these were opportunities disguised as difficult problems or situations or opportunities in disguise. However, we had to monitor this process accordingly, thus our Mortgage Officer, being familiar with these type documentation would have to make "surprised" visits with a Loan Officer to review loan mortgages packages prior to submissions.

Once again, we were developing a good reputation among other Majority as well as Minority Banks and other

Banking Institutions inside and out of the City and State. This included the investment banking community and at various meetings we were able to spend time talking about the various business opportunities that confronted us on a regular basis. There were such seasoned Bankers as Charlie Reynolds (Virginia), I O Funderburg (Atlanta, GA)| and others that shared information to our mutual benefit. On one occasion I remember one Banker telling me that their Bank could not afford to hire the kind of expertise that we had because it would be too costly. My response was that you need to make the hard decisions to bring in good talent because they will strengthen your Bank's bottom line. In reality "You cannot afford not to bring in the best talent available at some reasonable cost to your Bank for that also represents an investment in your future. Banker could no longer be caretakers of the "status quo", you needed someone that understood credit, banking operations and had some creative vision about where the industry was heading. It is simply good business sense to do just that. As our reputation grew as a Bank that was knowledgeable and could do some real creative financing of businesses, other opportunities begin to appear within and without our primary targeted market area.

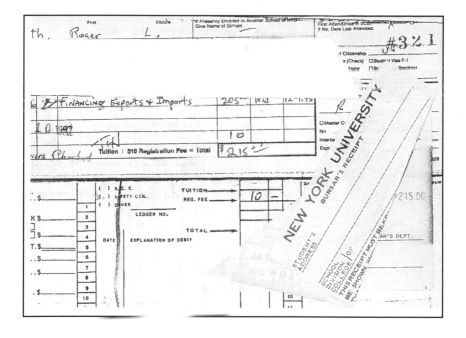

th. Roger L.

First   Middle   *If Presently Enrolled in Another School of NYU   First Attendance in SCE?
Give Name of School   If No, Date Last Attended:

#321

Citizenship
(Check)   ☐ Student Visa F-1
☐ Master C   ☐ Br   Resident

FINANCING Exports & Imports   205   W2   12-1-73   R

10397   10

ars Charged   Tuition | $10 Registration Fee = Total $215

☐ Master C
No
Interba
Expir

NEW YORK UNIVERSITY
BURSAR'S RECEIPT

$215.00

. . $ _____   ( ) S.C.E.   TUITION   10 —
( ) SAFETY CTR.
. . $ _____   ( ) OTHER   REG. FEE   10 —
K $ _____   2   LEDGER NO.
J $ _____   3
T. $ _____   4   TOTAL
. . $ _____   5   DATE   EXPLANATION OF DEBIT
. . $ _____   6
. $ _____   7
8
. $ _____   9
10   10

STUDENT'S ADDRESS

SCHOOL DIVISION OF COLLEGE

THIS RECEIPT MUST BE SHOWN   AR'S DEPT.

Chapter 5

Plan your Work and Work your Plan

NOTING IN THIS EXCITING CITY, THAT all work and no play made for a dull work environment, so we found a good mix of work and play. New Year's Eve Celebrations become an exciting time in this City. On numerous occasions, several of us, as couples, got dressed in our tuxedos and gowns would then drive into the City in our luxurious Mercedes automobiles, park in a secured lot, have a limousine pick us up for a fantastic night on the town of sightseeing, dinner and dancing. I remember on one occasion, I knew the chief/ owner of a small exceptional restaurant in Midtown on the Lower Eastside of the City and we were invited to dine there with a small group of about 20 guest couples. The Restaurant was closed to the public and the Chef provided a fine cuisine of a 12-15 course meal with all the trimmings including Champagne. We topped it off by attending a Birthday Bash at a plush well-known night club frequented by notable entertainers and movie stars, on this occasion they were honoring the singing duet, Ashford & Simpson. We arrived at the fenced-off roped entrance in our stretch limo where the crowd was held back by club security. As we exited and walked along the carpeted walkway with our friends, Regg and Julia, I could hear the onlookers calling out the names of various celebrities and entertainers and movie/television stars that they recognized but hesitated as we approached. They wondered who we were and they attempted to call some names that I didn't recognize but finally I heard someone say, I don't know who they are <u>but they must be somebody</u>! How excited I was to know that we were "<u>somebody</u>" in THE BIG City! There were other great celebrations on New Year's Eve, at the Studio Club and other Clubs and restaurants that were popular during those times. Even on several occasions after a night out on the Town or partying, we would stop by Junior's Deli in the wee hours to get a snack before heading home or after attending a concert such as ; Ray Charles performing at a well-known entertainment Center in the City due to the courtesy of a friend and promoter, Bill, we would have other guest come to our house for breakfast and perhaps even sleep over. Once at a Ray Charles Concert we were so close to the stage of his performance that we could actually hear the artist cursing when, I assumed that a musician would hit the wrong key, sometimes he would even stop playing mid-stream and restart the song from the beginning after taking corrective action. This was the "Maestro. …genius" at work. At one of our home-celebrations, a friend plus a noted jazz musician and writer accompanied us after a night out and performed for us and our guest on our Baby Grand Piano until the wee hours of early morning, much partying and the high-life existed during these times.

Then there was another occasion when "Ole Blue Eyes"

himself, the incredible smooth voice of Frank Sinatra at the Garden Center in New Jersey, performed. We were special guest of a fantastic couple, good friends of ours from a neighboring town in New Jersey. At the start of the concert we walked down to our seats escorted by the usher so close to the front that I thought that we were going on stage. Wow, we were a young Black couple but we knew the magnitude of our presence at that historical moment. How many people have actually seen the Master perform in his home State of New Jersey, I wondered? There was ice skating also at a midtown Center during the Christmas season in front of the giant Christmas Tree with a gathering crowd overlooking us on the ice. The fun times just kept coming, a good friend, Jim from back home in South Carolina introduced me to skiing when I initially arrived in the City some years ago and I fell in love with the sport. Immediately, after my first trip to a Ski Resort upon returning I was so excited that I went out and bought all my ski equipment the very next day. I love the sport and I thank him for introducing me to that exciting sport of skiing.

I realized early on as I arrived that since snow was common and routine in the winter season there that I needed to keep busy. I am eternally grateful to him for that introduction.

I began at each winter season to take a number of different groups to the slopes to introduce them to this exciting sport of skiing. On numerous occasions, I would take some couples on a short drive to The Playboy Club in New Jersey for some light skiing, for beginners plus entertainment and fun. Even some married couples got into the fun, we would plan trips to introduce new people to the activity and travel to the various lodges for excitement in Pennsylvania, the Poconos and Upstate New York.

When the winter Olympics was held in Upstate New York, I went up there to ski just before the big games started on my way to Canada. To my surprise there was no snow to be found anywhere. I came to realize that entire communities and their economies are based on snow during this time of the year and especially during this Winter Olympic event. I encountered a mechanical problem with my Mercedes and called the toll free 800 number and they directed me to the nearest Dealer to correct the problem. Satisfied and road worthy again, I drove on up to Canada before finding snow while a bit icy, but it served the purpose for the time being. I made frequent trips to Canada because I had met a friend while in Europe on vacation that lived in Montreal. Actually, we had met on a cruise down the Rhine River from Germany to France but did not get together until we met again in Amsterdam enjoying the nightlife of the City. During ski season, I would travel up to visit often. On my way back home it began to snow and all was well for the big contest, the games were ready to begin, let the games begin, GO U S A.

On one ski-trip occasion my wife canceled out at the last minute and co-incidentally the husband of the other couple cancelled. I enjoyed skiing so much that I was determined to go anyway. This wonderful marvelous couple of a viable thriving business that I had met through the Bank, recruited them and gave them a line of credit to fund the contracts they were getting for their very successful business. They were supposed to join us on a ski trip with another couple but things changed abruptly and only the man's beautiful wife and I ended up going together. We debated the issue and decided not to go into the mountains to ski but to a resort area and spend the weekend with a Motown Super Show featuring the Temptations' and nightclub in the town. Instead that is what we did based on that change of plans, we arrived at the Resort and the valet took our luggage and car as we departed inside like celebrities. We arrived just in time for a Dinner/Show with great seats and throughout the performance the entertainers were so captivated by the young lady's, my guest's beauty that they sang to her most of the night. Wow, I felt like a king and she was certainly the Queen and Bell of the Ball. After the show and dinner, things went a lot different than I had anticipated, we just enjoyed the evening, communicated about our perspective marriages and fell asleep. This was before the era of cell phones, therefore much of these things could not happen today. The next morning our spouses realized that just the two of us were out together and that we were not where we should have been and all had not been as I had portrayed things to be. Although we both had remained true and faithful to our marriage vows, ill feelings had forbidden any further involvement with either of them. I was truly saddened because they were really nice people and I mistreated and truly disrespected my position at the Bank and their relationship.

I was hopeful that they could move past this apparent indiscretion mostly on my part for they deserve better than what I had presented to them. The husband confronted me as a man should face to face and I sincerely respected his behavior and the confidence that he displayed in his wife and marriage. I sincerely regret my conduct in this situation and apologize to the both of them for my indiscretion. Things were not supposed to happen the way they did, nothing was planned, things just spiraled out of control very quickly, it was all my fault. Fortunately, this was my scandalous past not indicative of my future.

While it may appear that all that happened was fun and games, that was simply not the whole story at all. This City was a place that you worked hard and once the work was completed, you would take the pleasure to play hard as well. During my first year or so at the Bank, I worked late at nights and on weekends when the Bank was closed. While I got positive results from my work, it was simply because I worked harder than most, late nights and weekends preparing for the difficult task and hard decisions to be made during the regular work week days. Routinely on Monday mornings, I had prepared work assignments for all the staff to get done for the entire week. I had to work extra hard to accomplish these many tasks and others in promoting the Bank and keeping it operating smoothly and on sound footings.

Usually my wife was not sympathetic due to my working extra hours in an attempt to successful and prosperous and since I had proven to be untrustworthy, she probably thought that I was fooling around with other women most of the time. I played the field and joked a lot and people didn't realize how serious I took things because of my care-free demeanor. Again, I believed that I had proven a lot because I was successful at many levels of employment beyond most my age and short work history. Therefore usually when I worked on weekends, she would insist that I take our only son at that time, young Bryon, who was about 5 or 6 years old at the time. I would use this time to take his tricycle with him to the Park while I would roller skate and he would ride his trike. On one occasion, we stopped at a traffic light and since I wore my skates in the car while driving, at the red signal on the street corner where I would jump out of the car and skate around it several times spinning and doing backward turns and get back into the car in time to move on a green signal. I recall on one occasion, Diana Ross skated past us near the Park. By this time I had upgraded to the big Mercedes the 450 SE, where my son could stretch out in the back window for a quick nap. This time together also gave us the opportunity to visit the Zoo, the Garden for cartoon shows of Loney Tunes, Sesame Street and Circus events and other fun outings. Sometimes we would even invite a friend of his from The Chad School to join us for the excitement, little Milton was his favorite pal back then. We continued these outings and many times other exciting events would take place, many of those you could not do safely in these times. I am so thankful that God was with us even then.

Chapter 6

Attitude is Everything

WEEKEND WORK BECAME NECESSARY BECAUSE AFTER joining the Bank I realized that employees didn't have specific duties or job descriptions identifying their work assignments. Early on after joining the Bank as I was working at my desk on several assignments and I would notice employees running back and forth by my office with stacks of paper in hand appearing to be busy doing something. On occasion I would ask some of them what they were working on and their response would be somewhat confusing. I decided to have the Secretary give me all the mail for the entire Loan Department for a period of time. Therefore, I would review all the incoming mail for the department and maintain all the mail on my desk, yet the staff kept up their brisk pace of going back and forth with paperwork in the hands. I wondered what could they be working on because I had all the important departmental work on my desk. From this pile of work, I started to develop job descriptions and individual assignments and duties. I would assign certain people to individual task and write a memorandum outlining the specific task to be done. These memos gave me a method to monitor the work load of each individual and their effectiveness on getting their job done in a timely manner. Some Senior Banking Officer got upset with my writing these memorandums and didn't see the point of my using them to get work done. He reasoned that if I had time to write all these memos that I could get more done myself. Their existing method was to copy a letter from someone, make a hand written note on it and pass it along for execution. Obviously that procedure wasn't working, too many things were falling between the cracks and not getting done and upsetting customers. In addition, that procedure offered no ability to follow-up on the particulars in which a Bank Officer would have to respond to its status eventually.

As we began to change the opinion of customers and the Community at large for the better even the employee's attitude and pride kicked in regarding their work performance and confidence in their ability to complete assignments on time. While I had to put in extra hours on the job myself, even on Saturdays and sometimes on Sundays to get ahead of the work flow and stay on top of designated assignments. In this City that is said it never sleeps, the rules although unwritten was that you <u>work hard first</u> then <u>you play hard. This</u> rule I adhered to and was in full compliance. Notably I wasn't one to break that rule, as a matter of fact I endorsed it wholeheartedly or co-signed in with it. This was the time of my life for a guy in his twenties and doing it big in this City, "if you could do it here, then you could do it anywhere", was the cry of the town! And I was doing it big time.

During this period, I had a cousin that had relocated to the City to live and I felt that it was my obligation to show him the ropes, the night lights and fun life of the city as someone had done for me when I first arrived there. We hung out routinely at several clubs including the Playboy and Copa around the corner. I recall on one night we were partying there and a popular singing group at the time, The Friends of Distinction group was performing there. However, at break time, we invited one of the female entertainers to join us at our table. Things were going very well until suddenly a different subject came up by someone else in the Club, unknown to us, that prompted our immediate exit. Maybe it was someone who thought that they knew us, but didn't but certainly made us very uncomfortable so we left abruptly. One can never get too comfortable in the big city even at celebration times, when things appear to get a little out of control, you don't wait for something to happen, you just move quickly. That's what we did to avoid any conflict. Since we were two young brothers balling, it was time to go and not get caught up in any mess. Although in the City, we never had any real issue with anyone except an occasional tow truck showing up because of my illegal parking. I had a tendency to park almost anyplace because driving a big Mercedes in those days, I felt that I had special parking privileges to park almost anywhere as it was my "right of passage". On one occasion, on the East Side of Manhattan at a new Club had opened, I had double parked and went inside to scout the place and came out as a tow truck had my car hooked up and hoisted to be pulled away. I came out just in time and jumped on my car and stood up on it yelling and screaming at the driver. I drew so much attention that the crowd joined in with my anger and also started to shout and the tow truck driver released my car in due haste and drove away.

Not only was The Bank progressing well, my professional life was exciting and looking promising and my personal life was moving forward fast. My wife was graduating with her Master's Degree, we were expecting our 2nd child and we were buying a new house. Life was gooood! Unfortunately, as things progressed well, certain others may not always share your good fortune or feel that you are not so deserving of such good fortune. Some may have thought that maybe we even took our situation to view ourselves better than some others. As things progressed and our financial condition improved, I bought jewelry, furs and even another German car as well as had purchased a newer house in a more exclusive community. I recall on one occasion all of the executives were going out on a for dinner and we rode in my car and as the coats we were being placed in the trunk of the car. I believe that my wife had the only fur coat in the group and one of the executives wives simply said you may throw my "rag" anyplace, inferring that her coat was not a fur. So there was envy, jealousy and even an attempt at retribution on some issues. This was a hint of things to come.

We were bonding together beautifully, the staff, Officers, employees and even customers because profitability has far-reaching benefits and attitude adjustments. The working atmosphere was more pleasant, the attitude of workers was more pleasing to the customers in their transactions of business. I started to have specific employees specializing in certain type of transactions. I assigned one employee to handle one major account and all of its activities and we met periodically to discuss results and findings. There had been a problem had been created with a major depositor that had been an issue for several years and with no resolution apparently in sight to address the major issues on the reconciliation of deposit balances. In this particular instance, I inherited this issue and devised a system to attempt to resolve the problem. I decided to assign a particular employee to that account to work solely on its resolution and it was working beautifully, life was good.

When I first arrived there, I reviewed the files of key staff members and it was brought to my attention that several had issues that were very difficult to resolve. These issues were presented for me to handle and I received them with the assurance that I could resolve them in due time. The first person was perhaps Officer material however, he lacked the necessary skills to fit within the structure of the Bank operations. In this city there were many organizations like the American Management Association "(AMA)" which offered seminars for executives of Companies to enhance their skills and abilities. I found a seminar suitable for this individual, but he refused to take the 2- day session. The employer usually pays for the education of these executives and I had the benefit of taking several of their courses myself with great results and beneficial to the employer in my duties. I consider these courses valuable assets for growth companies and its employees looking for advancement. As I recall two of the courses that I took was Export / Import Financing and Account Receivable Financing. Both of these provided information essential to any lending officer, therefore I had first-hand knowledge of the effectiveness of these sessions. I insisted that he take this course and made it a prerequisite for his continued employment there. Naturally he took the course and later advised me on how it helped him progress although at another company.

There were several other employees that I had to enroll in some of the seminars that were taught and all made a tremendous difference in their work performance, confidence and attitude. The person that I assigned the key depository account took a course and it benefited our handling of that situation and others. There were various employee issues that had been ignored but as each employee opened up with me regarding their concerns with the Bank and their position as an employee. We were able to arrive at a solution some in which I made various promises to them for corrective actions. In one particular incident, I made a commitment to make a key employee an Officer of the Bank, while doubts existed, they adhered to my pre-conditions as to what results had to be achieved in order for that to happen. Most others just wanted more money and I responded with those request by saying that, first the hard work had to be done in order to achieved rewards for a job well done, that could and would be realized by their performance evaluations. The Bank was on a record earnings pace for the year, an historic highest in the Bank's history or any Black in the Nation. We all were working together to make this possible, it appears that all targeted goals were within reach for everyone to benefit.

Since many others were concerned about job descriptions, work performances and evaluations, all these matters had been addressed adequately. After those job descriptions then came the evaluations based upon them for most of the employees and this was an important issue for them to understand how the pay/reward system worked. However, one in particular was so upset over this issue that he had discussed seeking an attorney for corrective action. After meeting with others especially all those in my department, I was able to provide each and every one of them with performance reviews that they could understand and relate to in the performance of their duties. Many were rewarded and their duties were expanded from time to time as directed by their supervisor. The Bank was moving forward in a very positive and professional manner in which everyone knew what was expected from them and how they were to be rewarded accordingly. Things were all good.

Chapter 7

Everyone's Success is a Win -Win

THE ENTIRE COMMUNITY WAS PROGRESSING WELL with the Bank being the catalysis for that growth and development. During this time the neighborhood entertainment Theater was closed and in the process of changing ownership. Later we would entertain a proposal to fund acquisition and renovation of the structure. Therefore, we became the main drawing card and focus of activity on that important strip in Uptown. Many Community Leaders would stop by for a visit to chat about their plans for their Church and community projects. Further, I had the opportunity to visit perspective customers to solicit their business. In one office building that I visited, I noticed in the hallway as I passed Entertainment star, Stephany Mills. Wow, was I surprised of how short she was but excited just the same. On another occasion, in another building, I was visiting the next door tenant was Luther Vandross, I didn't get invited in for a visit but just being that close was a thrill. All these events happened right around Columbus Circle area near 59th street, an active business area to meet and solicit new clients.

Yes, many was looking to identify with the Bank' success in some way, whether visits, meetings, opening accounts or even just posing for pictures in front of the Bank building. We were riding high on <u>adrenalin</u>, performing well; emotions were high and under control, excitement was brewing and we were making positive news releases. Even our Officers were making news in various print media's such as Jet and Black Enterprise magazines, the local Community Newspaper and other print media. Emotions were high because the Bank was extremely profitable compared to its prior history. The Bank's performance was on record settings earnings and the primary reason was my area, the Loan Department's output. I was personally excited because this would mean that I would be able to reward some good employees for their hard work and sacrifices they had made and as a follow-up to my commitment to them. I had already kept some promises made to some specific persons such as promotions and salary adjustments and this would be similar to a cherry on top of an already great year by earning bonuses. Finally, I was able to show those employees in the entire department some financial form of appreciation. All were rewarded generously by my breakdown of the bonus allocations for the Loan Department.

Considering that I was the primary catalyst for the Bank's top earnings performance, I just knew that I was in for a banner large bonus check. I had simply reasoned that since it was my efforts mostly that had made everyone a success by the Bank's bottom line. As I waited for my envelope, one of the Senior executives came into my office and gave to me my bonus check. I didn't open it right away since I was focused on tmaking the Christmas Holidays exciting and the best ever for the staff. I sit at my desk relaxed and opened the envelope a little later but then to my surprise in horror, my bonus check was actually less than what I had given some members of my staff. As I reflected on the work that I had done and the sacrifices that I had made for the Bank since my arrival there to get it in the position that it had become financially; none of this had happened prior to my arrival, this type of success had not been achieved by any previous management team; setting up policies for lending, developing formats for reporting on loan approvals and problem loan reporting to the regulatory authority, recruiting and hiring qualified loan staff, formulating and developing marketing and job descriptions plus incorporating profit planning strategies instead of operating on a budget format and resolving issues that had plagued the Bank for years. My anger and resentment reached a high boiling point and I decided that a face to face confrontation was necessary. Although I had been totally professionally since my arrival there setting an example for those younger banking executives and I was still leading by example. Therefore, I composed myself before going into his office but I was ready to get physical, the street country boy ghetto was about to burst out of me. I walked in very calm but quickly got to the point of the amount of my bonus check. Upset and angry, that I threw the check in his face and asked "what in the hell is this? You know that I deserve the lion's share of any bonus allocation to the Senior Officers. Take this check and shove it …. I told him angrily. Of course, I was even prepared to go a couple of rounds fist to fist but I am glad that it didn't come to that. He responded that it wasn't his fault and he was planning to go to bat for me to get a larger amount, however now based upon my reaction, he would no longer do that. I had noticed all along in previous periods, that he had a problem with me because we both knew that although he was my superior, I was a much more a seasoned banker, smarter and with more thorough banking experience. I told him that he had screwed me for the last time and he would not have any future opportunities to do that again. I further told him that it was obvious that he needed the money more than I did in order to take such inappropriate type of action. I was doing quite well financially with the many toys and I along with a good friend of mine had recently traveled to the Poconos to purchase a lot to build a cabin for vacation spots in the future.

I knew from that moment that my journey at that particular Bank was over and had come to an end. I immediately incorporated myself as a business and formed an equipment leasing company and made contact with a major grocery chain in the area. Under the Minority Business status, I was to provide equipment to scan groceries for their stores and discount those leases to fund the purchase of the equipment. I was prepared to put the experiences of the Bank behind me even though I had met some nice folk and had made some good relationships there, many of which I would be eternally grateful for their loyalty, support and hard work that made success possible for us all. I realized that although my future at that Bank was over, there were some significate achievements and accomplishments that I was very proud of achieving there and that many had experienced and broaden their own options and had become a significant part of the Bank's history. I believe that many of the employees were encouraged that a brighter future would lie ahead for them due to their experiences there during that time. I was prepared to become an entrepreneur and take my talents to the open market. While somewhat disappointed, I was ready to turn the page into a new chapter in my life and career and thank GOD for these many blessings.

Rev. Roger L. Smith
November 4, 2007
Tell It Like It Is
Jonah 3: 3-5

Chapter 8

On to the Mountaintop

LATER ON AS I WAS PREPARING to leave work one day, I was introduced to a new employee that was recently hired as another Senior Officer, who was to be my boss, in other words to become another supervisor between myself and my immediate supervisor another layer or new level of management. In a sense, I was being demoted and this was how I was being repaid after taking the Bank off life-support and placing it on top of the mountain of success. I guess that I should not have been surprised at any of the actions taken after all desperate people do desperate things, at times of extreme uncertainty. My leaving would definite enough so provisions had to be made just in case I had to be fired, the department wasn't large enough to maintain two Senior Officers. In other words, my leaving would also place new and different responsibilities on one who already lacked the skills to maintain the pace that the Bank found itself in financially. They proved to be even less honorable than even I had even imagined, not all but certainly a few in charge. I had operated within the proper protocol of corporate management, reporting all my actions and changes to my immediate uplink which in turn made him look good and effective. I didn't sneak around behind his back and declare that these ideas were all mine nor report the success of the changes that I made to others because I was certain that everyone knew that none of those improvements took place before I arrived there. I had several meetings with the new Officer to be in charge of the Department, they were very cordial and he was very complementary of all that I had been able to accomplish there once he had the opportunity to review the operations at the Bank. Unfortunate people of ill-will can destroy your motivation and drive at an enterprise, as is sometimes the case therefore he didn't stay there long after finding certain attitudes prevailing there as well. I was pleased to leave this chapter of my life and move on to the next phase although unknown and uncertain at the time.

Unfortunately, while I had built a viable loan portfolio to help make the Bank extremely profitable, business loans require supervision, in other words, they must be managed. In personal loans or lending to individuals, you get a payment book to remit periodic loan payments until the loan is paid in full. However, phase two of the training of the Bank loan personnel, loan officers had not been completed prior to my leaving which effects the repayment ability of these type loans. Business loans require routine financial reporting to monitor the progress of the business that are to be analyzed for review, also an occasional visit to the company is required to observe the operation and note certain conditions of the business, number of employees on duty, cleanliness of the facilities, production schedules and other details that must be seen and noted. This process usually require two loan officers present, one a senior loan officer the other a junior loan officer in training what I had in the plans for the Bank. Further, there may appear questions that derive from the information developed from the review of the financial statements. Perhaps, phase two training never took place after I left the Bank, however I have no knowledge of who or when this additional training was done, if ever done. In business loans when the payment is missed, it's usually too late to take corrective action. This is another reason to monitor the bank account of the borrower, therefore if the balances are much lower than traditional amounts, this may indicate certain problems. Once the issues are determined and a corrective action proposed, then a possible restructure can be done of the loan to better fit the current dilemma. Otherwise you jeopardize the loan status and repayment when you don't follow-up on the required or established procedures in servicing these loans this is a practiced procedure when making business loans and that I included as part of the administration in writing the Loan Policy.

Realizing that my career at the Bank was over, I initially became bitter and somewhat sadden due to the manner of how it was ending. It appeared that the enemy or adversary had won. While I had other avenues on the horizon, you never know how things might work out. Especially now that I had a family that needed me to be a strong provider, and continue to provide the lifestyle that they had become accustomed to living. Now that I am a Christian, I have come to realize that the GOD that I serve will not leave nor forsake you, especially if you are operating within the plan and will of GOD and trying to do his will or the right thing and reside under the prayers of a faithful Christian Family. The pit that others dig for you will ultimately be filled by themselves because they will fall into it.

Suddenly out of the nowhere, it seemed, another blessing and God's favor, I received a call from a National head hunter, a corporate recruiter looking for a seasoned banker to be the President of a Bank in the Midwest. He advised me that my name was mentioned as a possible candidate and this information should be kept confidential. He asked me to direct him to an Officer in the Bank to speak to as a reference on my behalf. I instantly referred him to a Vice President, whom I respected and admired his expertise in the field. Things were moving along quite well and I was invited out to the Bank to meet with the Board of Directors. I arrived there and was met by a driver who had been assigned to transport me to the Bank's Headquarters at the downtown location. There I met the Chairman and founder of the Bank and the other members of the Board of Directors. They were all professional business men and women that were accomplished in their own prospective professions which was very diverse from retail, academia, construction and real estate. They were somewhat familiar with my background from other Bankers, community persons, Bank customers, clergy and others, as I found out later. Dinner was served in the Board Room and I was impressed, delighted and pleasantly surprised that dinner was served in silver with gold trimmed serving dishes and fine china and place settings.

After several days of reviewing the Bank's financials and audit and examinations reports, we got in negotiations for the position of President. Finally, before I left that city, I had a contract in hand for that position as President. Immediately upon arriving back home, I took the agreement to my personal friend, an attorney, who advised me to make the move and I accepted, signed and returned the contract which included a nice salary increase plus bonus, moving expenses plus other perks including a car and driver. I was most excited to come into work at my present employer, the Bank and resign my position there and announce that I was leaving to become President of another Bank. Oddly, upon my initial announcement to the Bank, a Senior Official, responded by saying that he knew all along that I would be the first to leave as the next Bank President of another Financial Institution Wow, I could not believe my ears, I wondered why he had not expressed that type of confidence in me and my abilities before then. In any event I was on my way to greener pastures but little did I know that the drama from this Bank was not yet over. However, I was reminded of a Bible scripture that said the thing they meant for evil GOD transformed it to good. Wow!

After arriving at my new place of employment and performing a few miracles regarding the Bank's operation in several months. I was summoned to report to the Chairman's Office which I promptly responded. After arriving there, he told me to take a seat and then informed me that he had heard from an Officer of my previous employer, the other Bank, advising him not to keep me because of some unpleasant developments there at the Bank. The Chairman was a very astute businessman as well as an Attorney, and according to him they made no particular references to anything specific. He was aware that the particular Bank had not attempted to help him in any way before prior to my coming aboard and therefore stated that he was not interested in any of their issues. He wanted me to be aware of that particular event although I already knew the kind of person who was there and would stoop to any level to make himself look credible while attempting to discredit another. I knew that nothing was done there out of the ordinary or against the rules that I had written myself therefore I didn't give that call or that situation another thought. I would simply let them consume themselves with that "witchhunt" by diverting their scarce resources into this area instead of profit making activities. I realize that if you lack the ability to build success on your own merits, that you simply look to attempt to build your reputation by trying to tear down another's achievements. Unfortunately criticism has become a way of life by some especially those that don't do anything worthwhile themselves. All they do is criticize what others do and expect that criticism to propel them to success. Actually there are those even today who make a substantial living on criticizing the work of others.

In life I have come to realize that a number of different types of people exist. Some as, I believe that you take on a task, no matter how difficult, do your best and if success follows then you reap the rewards for a job well done. There are some others, who are less skilled, attempt to find fault or errors in others work and attempt to build their reputation on tearing down the accomplishments of others. When I joined the Bank initially I found some errors and mistakes created by previous personnel. I could have made a big issue, called the guy a thief or simply attempt to destroy his character. I, however, called the person in for a discussion, voiced my concerns of the violations and gave him time to correct the discrepancies which was done. That's how professions operate within the confines of professionalism and decency. You simply lose respect for those who put themselves above the objectives of the organization especially when you have limited resources, no need to waste them not pursuing avenues of profitability. One cannot consider themselves and their livelihood more important than that of the whole. No one piece is greater than the sum of its pieces as in the whole. This was proven by the success or failure of any Bank because ultimately several of the Officers moved on to become Bank Presidents themselves. The proof is in the pudding, this was

High Finance moving or going uptown with that type of investment activity making the Bank or banking at its best.

As history would have it, I became A Bank President at the tender age of 35 after only a little more than a decade in the field of Banking. Now isn't GOD good!!!

I apologize, somewhat, because this was intended to be a testimony of the Bank however since my life was so closely connected with that Bank and the success it achieved fortunately our testimonies are the same. I feel certain if that Bank had a voice, it would thank GOD for Roger Lee Smith as I thank GOD for that particular National Bank and for those who had the vision and those that carried that vision out and the many that benefitted because it once existed especially those that made it work the best. I salute you all and may GOD continue to bless you and the memories that we all share. Peace and Love!

Printed in the United States
By Bookmasters